FOREWORD

I first met Frank Melling when he recruited me to ride at his Thundersprint event. He wasn't a bit like most organisers and I took an instant shine to him. He's a real hardcore perfectionist though and I soon learned that everything had to be right. Second best was first in the losers' race!

We got to know each other really well as I rode in all the Thundersprint events.

That blossomed into a really strong friendship not only with Frank, but his lovely wife Carol too, over the last 25 years.

I wanted Frank to tell some of the inside stories about my time with Honda – the things you won't normally see in print.

As a racer himself, Frank understands racing in a way which most journalists don't. This is what has made the book special; it's a real inside story.

I have helped him every step of the way and I'm happy that Frank has captured the spirit of what was the golden age of motorcycle racing.

I hope that you'll enjoy the trip too.

Jim Redman

**Jim Redman MBE – Motorcycle Racer
Six Times World Champion and
Six Times TT Winner**

Jim Redman riding his 499cc Norton in 1958 at Brands Hatch.

He earned £50 start money and finished second to the 'King of Brands' Derek Minter, who was considered unbeatable.

JIM REDMAN – MAN OF STEEL

Here's Jim on the Manx – a bike which gave him so much success in Africa. The tucked-in style is unmistakeable – as is the focused look. It was win – or back on the boat to South Africa!

Jim earned his reputation as a fabulous racer on public road circuits.

Jim and Tom Phillis at Mallory Park in 1961. Both are on works Hondas. This was Jim's first year as a contracted Honda rider and he earned, in today's money, the equivalent of £140,000 from the factory – plus appearance and prize money from lucrative international events. Not too bad for a rider who had arrived in Europe as a complete unknown just three years earlier!

"I enjoyed the TT but touring round on a Manx Norton, looking at the scenery, was nothing like the pressure of having to win – which was always the case with Honda."

Despite being considered too tall and heavy for 125s, Jim was always brilliant in this class. Here he is leading Kunimitsu Takahashi and Mike Hailwood during the 1961 Ulster GP. They are all on 125cc Hondas.

Jim with a 305cc works Honda at the Winter International, held at Pietermaritzburg in South Africa. This is 1962. Riding these 'second tier' factory Hondas was essential for professional riders to make the most of their GP success.

Racing was always a family affair with the Redmans.

MAN OF STEEL

That Jim Redman is one of the true greats of motorcycle racing is indisputable. With six World Championship titles and six Isle of Man TT wins to his credit, as well as being both captain and manager of the Honda race team, Redman's record is incredible.

I must confess to a personal bias in assessing the career of this remarkable man. As a schoolboy I first saw Jim Redman from the grass banking at Oulton Park. In the heyday of this famous Cheshire race track, Redman battled it out with the top riders of his day, screaming his fabulous works Hondas through the climbs and cambers of this historic circuit.

On the track, Redman was my idol. Smooth, effortless and graceful, he made racing look so very, very easy.

In the paddock, it would have been easy not to notice the man at all. He wore the plainest of black leathers and a basic, silver, 'pudding basin' helmet.

There were none of the evocative designs which adorned the helmets of Mike Hailwood, Phil Read or Giacomo Agostini – not even a national symbol like those of Luigi Taveri or Jack Findlay. Simply, the basic work gear of a working racer.

Later in life, I came to know Jim sufficiently well to call him a friend – and that's a rare privilege. Unlike many who make the transition from fan to friend, I have come to admire the man even more. Truly, Jim is something very special.

He is also badly misunderstood – and easily so too. Still invariably smiling at 91 years old, a glance at Jim's reactions when he is misrepresented shows that he is not a man to cross. Forget the traditional images of the hard man: one look into Redman's eyes will reveal why, in a generation of

Continued on page 18

Tom Phillis was Jim's close friend, as well as his teammate, but he had to be beaten in every race.

Pressing on with his 250cc Honda at the bottom of Bray Hill. Jim was beaten by Derek Minter, also on a Honda four – and was not best pleased!

Before he joined Honda as a team-mate, Mike Hailwood was a fierce rival for Jim. Here, Mike is chasing Jim's Honda hard on a 250cc Benelli. They later became close friends.

Team meeting with Jim, Aika San (the Honda team manager) and Mike Hailwood.

Riding at international events which weren't GPs was so important to professional riders because Grand Prix organisers paid the absolute minimum to the stars.
In this image, Jim is battling his way round Cadwell on an old 'four'.

Brands Hatch, with its huge crowds, was always a big payday – especially for Jim who did a lot of winning.

In Australia, during the European 'closed season', Jim is chased by Kel Carruthers on a second Honda 4.

Whatever the event, Jim always wants to win.

heroic riders, he was considered to be the toughest of the tough: a man of steel.

Redman was not only a tough man on the track – he was as hard as nails off it. When he was at his peak, racers were treated little better than medieval serfs.

Jim explains: "I was angry and upset that the guys who risked their lives every weekend often did not have the money to eat properly and maintain their bikes safely – and yet the organisers, and the FIM, all lived and travelled in the lap of luxury.

"Riders were considered to be expendable and died regularly because no-one was concerned about their safety. I was determined to change the status quo on both fronts."

So Redman earned a reputation among organisers as a ruthless negotiator and a 'difficult' rider with whom to deal. By contrast, his contemporaries thought that he was the best there was and held him in great esteem.

Motorcycle racing is an incredibly competitive sport and winning praise from within your own peer group is very hard. Yet, eight times World Champion Phil Read said of Redman: "He was a tough rider and had to be beaten if you wanted to win GPs. He rode the Honda well and gave me a hard time."

Jim on the 250cc Honda four at Quarter Bridge during the 1963 Isle of Man TT. This image is interesting because it shows how hard the factory Hondas were worked. Just have a look at the dents and dings in the exhausts and fairing. These were working machines – not show bikes.

At the time, Jim was always the fastest starter of all the GP stars. His unique technique was to squeeze the front brake hard to hold the bike in place while he pushed right up to the second the flag dropped – then he released it for a rocket ship start.

Mick Woollett, himself an ex-GP sidecar passenger and later the guru of motorcycle racing journalists, remembered Redman fondly: "There's no doubt that he was in the top 1% of GP riders. Redman was tough and determined, and from the moment I first saw him ride at Brands Hatch I knew that he was a top-class rider. He was determined to win – and it showed. Finishing second just wasn't an option."

Yet, it could have been very different. Tragedy struck Jim when he was just 15 years old. Both his mother and father died within 20 days of each other and Jim became head of the family.

He and his sister Jackie kept the family together with a huge amount of effort, which saw Jim working all day as a mechanic and then evenings and weekends fixing cars at the side of the road with his 'Kerbside Motors'. It was a tragedy of epic proportions and worthy of a book in itself – and it made Redman what he is.

As the key breadwinner, he was forced to leave England because of impending military conscription. "I told the Army that I would happily join up – if they would support the family, but that there was no way this was possible on a squaddie's pittance. I wasn't going to see the family starve and so I got on a boat and headed for Southern Rhodesia (modern day Zimbabwe)."

That decision is a window on Jim's steely resolve.

"I stood on the stern of the ship and cried as I left England – my England, the country I loved."

Jim was probably the founder member of the Self-Preservation Society. Just one day after arriving in Bulawayo he was in work and a year later he had established his own bike business in partnership with his friend John Love.

At the same time, Jim began his apprenticeship as a professional racer, travelling between Rhodesia and South Africa, competing in the combined championships – winning the 350 title and coming second in the 500. Redman was good from the outset and was soon winning a lot of money; enough to fund an attack on Grands Prix in Europe – but only just.

After purchasing a second-hand van and two Manx Nortons, Jim had just £50 left to fund his season's racing. It was either win or starve!

Jim soon established himself as a hard but reliable rider – one who delivered the results.

At the Dutch TT in Assen in 1960, Jim's close friend Tom Phillis broke his collarbone. Tom was one of two riders competing on factory Hondas and in the brutal business of GP racing, when he couldn't ride, everyone in the paddock wanted his works machine.

Jim was in Tom's caravan following the accident and he said: "Look Tom, I'm real sorry but I've got to get in the queue for your ride. You know how it is…"

At that moment Kiyoshi Kawashima, the Honda Team Manager, came into the caravan and Phillis introduced Jim.

"This is the man you want on the bike."

And Mr Kawashima agreed.

The received wisdom was that Jim was too big and heavy for the tiny 125cc Honda but he proved the sceptics wrong.

Redman rode the bike to an incredible fourth place but then went on to an even greater achievement.

The other factory Honda was to be ridden by Bob Brown

but he had an accident – and getting badly hurt at GPs in this period was completely normal.

Honda wanted Gary Hocking to ride the bike. Hocking had a reputation for being the most intelligent of the GP stars and was already competing on 350cc and 500cc works MV Agustas so he knew all about multi-cylinder GP bikes.

MV found the deal acceptable but Hocking had a personal contract with Shell while Honda were locked tightly into an agreement with Castrol. Neither of the two lubricant companies would give way so Hocking couldn't ride the Honda.

The Dutch TT organisers weren't going to be helpful either. The regulations stated that a rider had to practise on the same make of machine they intended to race. The only rider who met this criterion for Honda was Jim.

He and Kawashima pleaded for Jim to be given just a couple of laps to familiarise himself with the 250cc bike but their requests were refused. The answer was blunt: either ride the bike – or don't: it's your choice.

So, Jim's practice on the 16,500rpm, four-cylinder Honda amounted to riding it from the Honda van to the start line: that was it.

The Honda wasn't easy to ride either. "The bike was bloody fast, and revved like crazy, but Soichiro (Mr Honda) had an obsession with very short wheelbases to reduce wheelspin and make the bike turn quickly – which it did. The downside is that it was a bloody lively thing – nothing like the armchair ride of a Manx Norton."

With immense skill and tenacity, Jim learnt to ride the bike during the race and brought the Honda home in eighth place. In doing so, his future with Honda was secured, although he didn't know it at the time.

Before the race Kiyoshi Kawashima, the Honda Team Manager, told Jim that if he just brought the bike back in last place he would get a test at Francorchamps the next week. When Jim stopped outside the Honda van, the team were ecstatic – and Jim was on his way with the factory team.

By Jim's modest standards, the money was good too. Jim received £100 each for riding the 125 and 250 – plus his prize and start money – a total of about £250. This doesn't sound very much but it was about the equivalent of £6,000 today.

The problem was that as soon as Tom Phillis was fit again there would be three riders for only two works machines.

Jim was very fond of Bob Brown and before the German GP at Solitude he said to his friend: "You know Bob, one of us is going to get fired. Tom was first in so he'll be okay but one of us two will have to go."

This was when Redman's grit kicked in because GP racing was a savagely tough way to earn a living. In the first practice, Jim saw a Honda parked at the side on the track with Bob Brown next to it. Redman stopped his bike and went across to help.

Brown was sat on the wall, next to his bike, and Jim asked how he was. The Australian said that he was fine but he had the most massive headache. At the time, all the riders wore cotton wool stuffed in their ears to give some minimal protection against the noise of the unsilenced engines. Jim noticed that blood was oozing past the cotton wool in Brown's ears and running down his neck.

"I had first aid training but I looked at the amount of blood and thought there was no way that I was going to take out the cotton wool. I'd rather be criticised for doing nothing than killing someone. It was just too much for me," said Jim.

"That night, Bob's wife came to our caravan and I asked how he was. She was very quiet and just said that he was dead. We were in a hard, hard business and if we'd allowed ourselves to be sad, we would have just cracked up. I was sad for Bob and his wife but I knew that it could be me dead in the next race.

"So I rode the 125s and 250s all season and I loved the bikes. I did well but there was no contract. I went back to South Africa wondering what I was going to do for the 1961 season. Then I got a telegram from Honda asking me to come to Tokyo and bring Marlene, my wife, and our new baby.

"The first thing that I did was to ring Tom – not easy or cheap in those days. He said that he'd got the same telegram so we'd better go. I asked him how much he was going to ask for from Honda to ride for them and he said he loved the bikes so much, he'd ride for free and just make the money with start and prize money.

"Even though I was desperate to ride for Honda, I still wanted paying! My heart was in my mouth because it took all our family's spare money to go to London and then Tokyo but it had to be done. Honda met us at the airport and looked after us really well.

"Then we met Mr Kawashima and he asked us how much me and Tom wanted to ride. To be honest, we didn't have a bloody clue. Tom was quick thinking and he said to Mr Kawashima, 'Can we discuss this tomorrow, please?'

"Mr Kawashima was happy with this so that evening we tried to work out a plan.

"We knew that Gary Hocking got £4,500 from MV and that John Surtees had £7,500 from MV so we thought we'd ask for £4,500 each.

"Neither of us wanted to say the actual figure in case we got thrown out of Honda for being greedy but in the end we decided I'd try. I blurted out £4,500 really quickly in case Mr Kawashima went nuts, so I could deny ever saying it.

"But he didn't. Instead, he went to a big wallboard and drew a line down the centre. On one side he put: 'Riders get £4,500, plus all start and prize money and bonuses from sponsors'.

"And on the other side, it was blank. Mr Kawashima said, 'Well, what do Honda get?'

"Tom laughed and said, 'You get two great riders.'

"And we all had a laugh and then shook hands. That was that. I was a Honda factory rider. In total, I earned about £7,500 during 1961 – that's around £140,000 today which was good money.

"Not that it was all profit though, because I paid all our travelling expenses and kept the family going. But there was an unexpected bonus – and a nice one too. I asked Honda if I could borrow a 250cc Four for the South African events, during the winter of 1960/61.

"At first they weren't keen but I told them that they could trust me. There would only be me touch the bike and I'd just put petrol in it – nothing else. I would guarantee that no-one would even look at the engine.

"It was an amazing machine, and a great credit to Honda, because the bike ran flawlessly for four events. I just cruised round like it was a road ride and left everyone else in the dust. Good times and the start of even more to come with Honda."

ASSEN 1964 – THREE GP WINS IN A SINGLE DAY

PART 2

In 1964, Jim achieved his legendary three GP wins in a day at Assen – an incredible feat. Phil Read, himself a great rider, is about to be passed by Jim in this picture.

Jim with the Honda at full chat winning the 350cc class at the 1964 Ulster Grand Prix. What a sight! What a sound!

Jim decimated everyone in the 1964 Junior TT race.

By 1964, Jim had the prestigious Isle of Man TTs under his total control, winning both the 250cc and 350cc TTs – and the World Championships.

"When I won the third GP at Assen I was so pleased and proud. I didn't stop smiling for a week."

THE GREATEST DAY IN GP RACING

Whenever motorcycle racing fans get together there will be an argument about the best rider, the greatest comeback or the finest race.

Agostini – 15 times World Champion and racing on public roads? Mike Hailwood – able to win anything, in any conditions and against any opposition? Rossi – beating the toughest racers on the planet and on equal machinery – must be the greatest of the modern era, but Vale has never won a TT…

For me though, one beacon stands out in the history of motorcycle racing. What greater achievement can there ever be than winning three Grands Prix in one day, on three vastly different motorcycles? This was Jim Redman's triple win at the 1964 Dutch TT.

To ride 500km (over 300 racing miles) and three hours racing in one day – and every second a battle for every inch of the track against the best riders in the world, is incomprehensible today.

This is how it happened.

First, a prologue: In 1964, Jim was not only Honda's top rider but also team captain and manager. In short, he carried a lot of responsibility. Jim tells the story: "I came to Assen following two wins in the Isle of Man. As far as I was concerned, I should have won three TT races but the throttle came loose in the 125 race, and Luigi Taveri, who was Honda's lead 125 rider, beat me by three seconds. I didn't win and that's racing.

"People said I was too tall and heavy for a 125 but I thought, 'Let 'em say what the hell they want. The results will show whether I can ride a 125 or not.'

"When we got to Assen it was baking hot – absolutely on fire! Luigi was injured in practice and out of the race, so Aika San (the Honda team manager) said I would have to ride the 125 and just keep Hugh Anderson, on the Suzuki, from taking too many points from Luigi.

"Aika San's idea was never for me to win but just to keep the Suzukis and Yamahas off Luigi. Luckily, the 125 race was my last race of the day so I

1965 was a brilliant year for Jim. He won the 350cc Junior TT at over 100mph.

could do the 250 and 350 races first, which were my main jobs, and then get on with helping Luigi.

"My real targets were the 250cc and 350cc races because Honda had given me the job of winning those two world titles. The 250 race was going to be tough because Phil Read was riding the RD56 Yamaha which was streets faster than my Honda four. The Yamaha was 15kph (10mph) faster down the straight than even my really quick 250 Honda four which was the best one by far that Aika San had provided for me.

"The 350 race wasn't a problem. The only real challenge was from Mike Hailwood and his four-cylinder MV. This was too slow and heavy to cause me any concern, even with Mike riding it.

"The 350cc race was first and then the 50s. This meant that I could have a bit of a break between the two races. Then there was the 250cc race which was going to be hard because Phil's Yamaha was so much quicker. I could have another break during the sidecar race and then there was the 125 class. As I said, my job was not to win but just to keep the Suzukis and Yamahas from taking too many points off Luigi and I told everyone this was what I was going to do. I made sure that the whole paddock knew this plan.

"But of course, this was not what I was really planning because I only ever raced to win. Right from the start, I was aiming to beat them but it was easier if everyone thought I was not going to ride to the limit. I often rode in all three classes at GPs. If the circuits were twisty enough to keep the distance under 500km we could ride all we wanted.

"You couldn't do it at fast circuits like Hockenheim, where you covered a lot of miles, so I only competed in two classes there.

"At Assen, the races were short enough to run for just under an hour and still stay under the mileage I just about kept under the 500km maximum racing distance for a whole GP. I knew it was going to be a tough day at the office but I was a professional motorcycle racer, and Honda works rider, so tough was what I expected. In my position, there were no easy days.

"It also wasn't anything particularly special to race 500km in a day. I did it. Other riders did it. We raced motorcycles for a job so that's what we did. Assen was no different from any other GP for me. Some top riders never used to have sex for ten days before a GP but that didn't suit me. I had no hesitation in this respect. They'd go up to Marlene (Jim's wife) and say, 'Yes or no?' Then they'd go away when Marlene always said yes.

"It was over 30 degrees as we lined up for the 350 race but I was very relaxed. I never did any physical training because I rode so much. I would start at over 100 races a year — anywhere where there was money to be earned and every weekend and sometimes mid-week too. A lot of racing, and sex, kept me very fit.

"A flag start is very different from starting with a clutch. The silence on the grid is deafening. You've fiddled with your goggles and got your gloves comfortable and the tension builds. Then you carefully pull the bike back on compression. With the Honda four it was tricky to get a piston actually at top dead centre by feel.

"You tense your legs and get ready to hurl yourself forward like one of those bobsleigh pilots. Then you watch the starter. You don't think of anything in the world — not the bike, your family, winning or losing or crashing. Your mind almost climbs on to the starter's flag — you're watching so closely.

"Everything goes into slow motion. It's like being in a different world. The flag moves very, very slowly and you push like bloody hell. All around you is an explosion of noise from unsilenced engines. It's like being in a war — but you don't hear anything as you would normally. Then, automatically, you know exactly when to drop the clutch. It's all just by feel with no computers or anything else to help. You know the perfect timing as much as you know how to breathe or walk.

"You know by touch and sense if the bike has fired, and you feed in the clutch and swing your legs over the bike in one movement, and then get your head buried in the tank. It's all one fluid movement — and you go from total silence stood at the side of the bike, to 13,000rpm and tucked in with just one smooth motion.

"The 350 race was straightforward. I led from the start and won by 12 seconds with Mike second, and Remo Venturi, on the Bianchi twin, a long way back in third. It was nothing special and I won at the slowest possible speed. I always aimed to win as slow as possible. No-one pays you extra prize money, or gives you bonus points, for lap records.

"I knew that the 250 race was going to be a lot different. The 250 race was considered to be the main race of the day because there were so many good riders and so many factory bikes. As well as me and Phil, Benelli had a quick four-cylinder bike ridden by Tarquinio Provini, and Mike Duff and Tommy Robb were on Yamahas. On paper there were plenty of potential winners but, in reality, there was only me on the four-cylinder Honda, and Phil with the disc-valved, two-stroke Yamaha.

"The flag dropped and we screamed off the start line together, and I knew that this was going to be one hell of a race. Even though it was a public road, the Assen track had a lot of grip and neither of us would give an inch. We were both hard riders and neither of us was frightened of anything, so we were close to banging into each other on every corner and flat out at over 130mph. I was determined to win that race and nothing was going to stop me.

"The problem was that my four-stroke Honda was 10mph slower than Phil's two-stroke Yamaha so, for a lot of the race, I had to slipstream just to stay with him. The 1964 Honda was the last of the fours and we weren't supposed to rev the bikes over 13,500rpm but I took it to 15,000rpm in every gear, just to stay with Phil. I had complete faith in Honda, in Aika San and Nobby as my mechanic.

"On the last half-lap, I out-braked Phil time and again. Phil braked on the inside of the corner at the end of the back straight and I just rode right round the outside of him, right on the limit but in control. I was riding absolutely on the limit but never stupidly. The key thing was that I expected to win and I believed that I could. No bullshit, I knew that I was going to win. It was just a matter of doing the job. I never thought about crashing or not winning,

"The problem was that Phil's Yamaha out-accelerated the Honda on every corner. I was going to have to do something different. As we approached a fast chicane I decided that if I could get through it without lifting my chin off the tank, I could carry extra speed on to the finishing straight to win. It was a mistake, as the extra speed caused the back wheel to step out in a big slide and Phil went past again as I fought for control of the bike. I always raced with my brain and, to a far lesser extent, with my balls – so I really cursed my mistake.

"As we approached the second to last corner, I made up my mind that wherever Phil braked I would go down the inside and pass him. I had to change down two extra gears to try and stop for the corner and when I cracked open the throttle, the bike surged forward with the rev counter needle two or three thousand revs over the limit.

"I had no time to worry about the bike blowing up because I had no choice. If I changed at 13,500rpm I was going to lose and if it blew up I was going to lose, so it either took the extra 3,000rpm and stayed together – or didn't. Second place was not an option.

"When I saw how well this had worked I did exactly the same on the last corner. As we approached the finishing line, I saw Phil coming up alongside and I knew that if I changed gear I would lose the race. I decided not to change gear and let the engine rev its heart out: if it burst I lost, and if I changed gear I lost, so I hung on and won – by one hundredth of a second.

"In those days, the bloke with the chequered flag used to stand on the track and he really panicked when he saw these two maniacs screaming towards him with their heads buried in the tanks. He jumped back somewhere a bit safer but my mechanic Nobby Clark, who was quick-thinking, rushed up to the finishing line and took a picture in case there was an argument about who had won.

"No-one will ever know what figure that motor revved to because the rev counter only read up to 18,000rpm and the needle was stuck there. And this was a bike I had never pushed over 15,000rpm before! What a little beauty that motor was. Aika San stripped it after the race and found nothing wrong but still replaced everything as every part must have been unmercifully stressed.

"During this last lap, Phil and I passed and re-passed each other no less than 12 times. We were way ahead of all the others, lapping the entire field, except for Tommy Robb in third place who was nearly three minutes behind. The lap and race records for this race were well and truly smashed!

"Once I got off the bike my legs felt like jelly and I could hardly stand up. It was like coming on to dry land after a bad ferry crossing. People were slapping me on the back, there were congratulations and smiles, the crowd was yelling. It all seemed so far away from me at that moment. I wanted only one thing – to collapse and be alone.

"When I got to the winners' rostrum I was met with a standing ovation, the press called it the race of the century, just as they had a week before in the Isle of Man. Nobby said to me: 'This is getting real rough, a race of the century every weekend.'

"In the shade of the Honda garage I lay spread eagled on the concrete floor because this was the coolest place we had. Not only was I melting physically but I was burning inside with the satisfaction of having ridden the race of my life and won, despite having a slower bike.

"I took down the top of my leathers and washed my face with Eau de Cologne, all the while thinking, 'I'm too old for this type of race. I don't ever want to have to ride like that again.'

"However, just an hour and a half later I had to be on the starting line for the 125 race, again with Phil and the rest as opponents – and I knew I could expect another very difficult race. I just lay on the concrete and tried to get a bit cooler. Everyone left me alone because they knew the state I was in. I had won two races and all that I could think of was whether I could get three in a day. Following team orders, and just riding for a finish, never crossed my mind.

"I knew Phil was just as exhausted and weary as I was. I heard that Phil was lying on his camp bed, a cigarette between his lips, and I knew that he was wishing the 125 race was over as much as I was, and he hadn't done the 350 race like I had.

"We walked slowly to the start line again as our bikes were brought out for the 125 race. For the public it was going to be an incredible race but for us riders it was a job that had to be done. However, very quickly, excitement had the adrenaline pumping: I didn't feel tired anymore and the aches and pains were gone. In their place now was a burning desire to win again. I was going to win and there would be no second place or riding for a finish.

"Phil Read took the lead because I made a terrible start – almost last away – but I was so keyed up from the 250 race that I just carved my way through the field from nearly last. I caught up and passed Hugh Anderson, Suzuki's top rider, who had made a good start. I had to barge past him on a tricky right hand bend, that normally I would have had more respect for, but I had to take big risks coming from the back if I was going to catch Phil.

"Once I caught Phil, I just sat behind him. Phil maintained a good rhythm, and in no time we'd left the others far behind. This time I had the extra speed and so waited for the right moment to overtake. With three laps to go to the finishing line, I saw a chance to go ahead. We'd just reached a slower group of riders and I shot past Phil and overtook them.

"Phil pulled out all the stops, taking all kinds of risks to try and pass me, but I knew it was too late for him: from now on he would not be able to do it. Racing is a lot in your mind. I knew that I could beat Phil and that was all there was to it. It wasn't being hopeful or confident but simply, absolute 100% certain that I was going to win. No bullshit or bragging – just total certainty that I was going to win.

"What I didn't want was a repeat of the 250 race – that had been too close for comfort and I had taken too many risks. I knew Phil wanted revenge, but I had the speed advantage, so I just got my head down and took off. I finished six seconds ahead of Phil, and smashed the lap record, with all of the first six finishers beating Hugh Anderson's old record.

"The increase in speed was thanks in part to Phil and me because our battle had carried the field along with us. Hugh Anderson, not known for throwing compliments around too readily, shook my hand warmly, saying, 'Brilliant, bloody brilliant!' His praise meant a lot to me since it came from an individual I respected immensely.

"The 125 race was the third of the day and it completed my hat trick. At the end of the day I was exhausted, but so satisfied: I had won three races and beaten six records. I was bone weary as I climbed the rostrum to stand on the top step again but I knew that I had achieved something that no man had ever done before: three GPs in one day, for a man too big for a 250 or 125!

"The crowd was wonderful and went crazy and you can imagine my feelings as I looked out over it, wondering could anything be better than this? Lots of riders would like to win three GPs in a lifetime and I had done it in one day! Although I was totally exhausted at the end of the race I was still pumped up.

"After a nice hot shower back at the hotel it was off to prize giving to collect all my trophies and enjoy the party. And it was a bloody good party too! I was the star and I enjoyed it. Loads of riders came up to me and there were a lot compliments. This meant a lot to me, and still does, because these were my fellow professional riders – and every one of them was bloody good in their own right. It was the best day of my life.

"Aika San and the Honda team were just as excited as me. I made sure everyone knew that if they hadn't done such a good job making the bikes for me, I could never have won. This meant a lot to them. I felt very fortunate to be a Honda factory rider and I wanted them to know what I felt in my heart.

"It wasn't PR or keeping sponsors happy like riders have to do today. I was just very grateful to Honda. I told them all how I felt, but especially Aika San, and all this was with the beer flowing and the party in full swing. We were more than a team. We were family and we had achieved something remarkable together. Afterwards, we went back to the hotel and I made sure that Marlene was looked after too!

"In 1995 I returned to the Dutch TT once more but, this time, demonstrating my old Hondas rather than as a racer. Kevin Schwantz was there and he said to me that he had heard what I had done in 1964 and that he was lucky to win three GPs in a year, never mind one day! Everyone should experience the euphoria of victory, in some part of their life, at least once."

JIM REDMAN – PROFESSIONAL RACER

"You have to remember that I was a professional racer.

Racing was what put food on the table for my family. Earning money wasn't a luxury – it was essential.

When I arrived from Rhodesia, I got my 350 and 500 Nortons direct from the Norton factory in Birmingham. They were ordered and paid for by my Rhodesian dealer on the Wednesday. On Friday of the same week I was at Brands Hatch, riding against the best riders in Britain.

I got £50 start money which was okay when a skilled tradesman was earning £12 a week.

I rode well and at the end of the meeting they put on a top twenty riders: I was included in this. I managed second, inches behind the winner.

Murray Walker, who was commentating, grabbed me in the pit lane shouting that it was Derek Minter, King of Brands Hatch, who was the only one who had beaten me.

I wasn't interested who it was. For me, it was just some more cash!

This was bloody good because before Brands, I only had £50 left in the world.

Once I became a Honda factory rider things got better but the GP organisers were still hard work – properly ruthless.

For the first GP of the 1962 season I'd become Honda Team Manager – as well as Team Captain. I went to see the organisers of the Spanish GP which was held in Montjuic Park on the outskirts of Barcelona. They were arguing over start money, which they always did, so I said to the Honda mechanics, 'Leave the bikes in the van until I tell you to get them out.'

The organisers said, 'You can't do that – no other team blackmails us.'

I told them that Honda had given me orders not to start under a certain minimum, which was bullshit but they weren't to know that, and we were Honda so pay up or we leave: and they did!

What used to make me really angry was that it was the riders risking their lives – and in every race there was a good chance of getting killed – while the fat bastards organising the events lived like kings.

I made sure that the riders got the best deal that I could get for them.

I used to say two riders were killed every month until a fan corrected me. The actual figure was a minimum of thirty a year.

I rode in as many non-championship events as I could because I could earn good money from them.

I could get £100 a bike start-money now that I had the Hondas, and £50 for winning a race, so a weekend at Brands, Mallory or Oulton could earn me £300 – and that was on top of my Honda salary.

The money wasn't for free though. It was tough racing and a lot of travelling. I had no need for all this modern fitness training. I got fit by non-stop travelling and racing!

The moment the European season was over, I had planned my winter racing – first South Africa and then Australia and New Zealand.

In 1963, I did fourteen races in New Zealand and won every one. I wasn't there for sightseeing!

Honda were very good to me. They loaned me either the works version of the 305cc twin that they sold, except that our bikes had trick, six-speed engines, or second string four-cylinder bikes.

I'd get the Honda factory mechanics to go through the loan bikes at a GP then I'd just ride them. I didn't do polishing or any other cosmetic bullshit. They were like my Transit vans – working tools which let me do my job.

We were always paid in cash – everywhere. This was sometimes a nuisance. Italian Lira notes were huge so I used to stuff them down my underpants because you weren't supposed to take money out of Italy.

This became a real nuisance because money was piling up everywhere. There were Deutschmarks, Dutch guilders, francs – all bloody sorts. I used to keep loads of cash stuffed in a shoebox in the front of the van.

Things were getting out of hand so my Honda teammate Luigi Taveri, who was Swiss, said he would get me a Swiss bank account. The problem was that Luigi lived near Geneva, in the north-west of Switzerland, and I wanted to get rid of my cash straight after the Italian GP at Monza, which is near the eastern edge of the country.

So, when I crossed the border into Switzerland I pulled up outside the first bank that I saw and walked in with my box of money.

I stuck it on the counter and when the young lady opened it she had kittens! I was taken to a private room to meet the bank's top man – Ferdinand Rhotembueler.

I told him where the money had come from and he was all smiles and said that he could get me 20% interest – which he did.

I brought him a lot more shoeboxes after that.

When I retired I had £100,000 saved up. That would be around £2.5 million today. Not a bad return for someone who arrived in Britain with £50 – but also a tragedy when I think of all the close friends who died during this wonderful period of motorcycle racing.

So that was the reality of life as a professional racer in the Golden Age of GPs."

Honda loaned Jim works versions of the 305cc Honda racer they sold over the counter. The bikes ran faultlessly and won a lot of money for Redman.

Jim at Mallory with Vittorio Carrano, MV Agusta works mechanic, and Mike Hailwood.
The non-championship International meetings attracted stellar entries.

Battling it out for good money at Brands Hatch with the 'King of Brands' Derek Minter, #11, and arch rival Phil Read just behind him. The Internationals were not demonstrations!

Jim with a typically well-worn – but still super-fast and reliable – Honda 4 being chased by Mike Hailwood on a 250cc FB Mondial at Scarborough.

Here's Jim in the torrential rain at the Ulster GP.
There were no off-days or conditions too dangerous for riders in the Golden Age of GP racing. Many died.

Jim was always very switched on with PR – long before public relations was invented. Being media-friendly boosted his pay packet.

HONDA 6

By 1965, the marvellous four-cylinder Hondas had become obsolete so the legendary '6' made its first appearances – and Jim won both the 250cc and 350cc TTs.

For anyone who heard a '6' being ridden hard, the noise was unforgettable.

"Honda called and asked me to come to Japan and test the new bike which was going to replace the four-cylinder bikes we'd been racing. I landed at Tokyo Airport and caught the Bullet Train straight to Suzuka. No messing about – I wanted to see what Honda had made for me!

"From the first moment I saw the '6' I thought that it looked brilliant – absolutely incredible. When I first heard the bike being warmed up, the hairs stood up on the back of my neck. The shriek of the engine was pure magic – a proper racing beast. There wasn't a sound like it. Not our fours or the MVs. The '6' was unique and I just couldn't wait to ride it. But things weren't that easy. By the time I'd left the pit lane on my first session I could feel it made a lot of torque and wouldn't be easy to ride.

"When I came back, I said to Aika San, 'It's too short!' Aika San pulled a longer swinging arm from behind him and said that he knew I would say that. The problem was that Honda San (Soichiro Honda) was very hands on and he had insisted that the bike should have a very short wheelbase – only 52in – to give more drive and make the bike turn quicker.

"As well as the longer swinging arm, Aika San said that we could move the front forks round to give us a longer bike. But whatever me or Aika San thought, it was Honda San's company and he was going to have the final say. By the end of the test we managed to knock the '6' into a semi-ridable bike.

"I said, 'Fuck it. Load it up for Monza and I'll ride it.' Honda San had been watching us test but didn't come into

Unfortunately for Jim, and every other World Champion of the time, a young Italian called Giacomo Agostini arrived on the scene in 1965. Jim was still the master though and Ago never beat him in a race where they both finished.

the garage until we were packing up. He came in and said, 'You're not riding that bike. You'll kill yourself.'

"I thought that he was going to stop us taking the '6' to Monza so I was well pissed off. But I said to Honda San, Monza only has five corners and everything else is long straights. I can blast it down the straights and then trickle round the corners. So he agreed that we could race it.

"To get the bike from Japan to Italy we had to pay for three extra passenger seats. The '6' was already a star! When we got to Italy, they let me through customs straight away and when I stood outside the airport I could hear the bikes already practising at Monza. As soon as I got on the track, I knew that the bike was right – it was just so fast. I could ride it too and I set pole.

"The weather was cool and damp during qualifying which suited the air-cooled, six-cylinder engine perfectly because it always ran hot. The following day it was scorching and the engine overheated and lost power. This let Phil Read win, and worse, Mike Duff on the second works Yamaha just squeezed past me on the last 100 metres. If it had been cool, they wouldn't have seen which way I had gone.

"The final GP of the year was at Suzuka – Honda's home track. We had a completely new frame and the motor had been fully sorted. I just loved that bike. The mistake that I made was buggering off and leaving everyone for dead – I won by half a lap in front of Phil Read on the works Yamaha. If I'd gone slower, then maybe Yamaha wouldn't have built the four-cylinder two-strokes which gave me so much trouble the following year!"

Jim after being presented with a piston from his beloved six-cylinder Honda.

NOBBY CLARK

Here's Nobby with the pit board signalling in the TT.

"**N**obby was a really skilled fitter and had worked for Rhodesian Railways, which were considered to be the best in Africa. He knew Gary Hocking and when Gary was getting lonely because he was spending so much time at MV Agusta, where they only spoke Italian, he brought Nobby over to Europe – more for company than a real job.

"Nobby paid for his own flight to the TT and then Gary helped him after that. When Gary went car racing, Nobby asked if he could help me out so we let him sleep in the van and Marlene fed him. Then Nobby would give the Japanese mechanics a hand doing the basic stuff, like lifting engines out of frames and cleaning stuff.

"At the end of the season, he asked me to see if Kawashima would let him go to Honda and stay in the single men's quarters and really learn about the race bikes. I said to Kawashima that I thought it would be a good idea, but it was quite a big deal to have a non-Japanese working on factory bikes so Mr Honda himself had to sign everything off.

"Nobby was a fine mechanic and I liked working with him. After I retired he worked on Luigi Taveri's five-cylinder, 125cc Honda and Luigi thought he was excellent too."

Nobby Clark was a fellow Rhodesian and the only non-Japanese mechanic in the team. Jim and Nobby got on very well.

THE SECOND COMING

Jim rode a vast range of different bikes on the revival circuit. He's giving a 750cc MV Agusta the beans here!

After retiring from GP racing, Jim has had a stellar career on the classic revival scene. Here he is at the Thundersprint in 2011, riding Clive Brooker's CR750 Honda – and still 100% racer.

Jim is endlessly patient, kind and appreciative of his fans – an absolute star!

After leaving the world of racing, Jim had a number of business ventures, ranging from dude ranches to importing bikes and even race horse breeding. But the call of the race track was still strong and, in 1995, Jim had his comeback race, winning at Daytona on the ex-works MV3. "I had a grin for six months after that..." remembers Redman.

The Daytona win did something else for Jim: it reminded him that race tracks were really the place he could truly call home. Almost by accident, he set off on a replica of his continental circus days travelling the world wherever there was a classic bike meeting which interested him – and this is how I got to know him.

Everyone in classic racing knew that Jim was hugely popular with race fans of all ages so eventually I plucked up the courage to invite him to ride at the then-fledging Thundersprint, an event which my wife and I owned. In the process, I learned a lot about the man.

It took me three hours of pacing up and down, watching Jim entertain at the Manchester Bike Show, before I had the nerve to ask him to ride with us. When I did, I was in for a real shock. Here was one of the greatest names in motorcycle racing talking to the organiser of a small classic sprint held, then, at a highly unfashionable northern kart track. Truly a case of the man who had seen and done everything, talking to the organiser who had achieved almost nothing.

Lots of things could have happened. A curt dismissal. A patronising rejection or perhaps, at best, even a diplomatic excuse. In fact, the result was completely unexpected. Yes, Jim would ride with us and yes, he wanted paying – on the nail. But once we had an agreement, we got the same care, thought, effort and sheer professionalism that has been his hallmark as a racer.

In the 15 times Jim rode for us he never once let us down in any way.

Book an appointment with a journalist – Redman is early. Leave him with a sponsor – he does a faultless job of promoting not himself, but the event. Introduce him to a politician and he has the easy grace and confidence of the true superstar.

But best of all, Jim has infinite patience and courtesy with his fans. No question is too basic, no story repeated too often not to be told again, no request is too trivial for Jim to satisfy. Everyone who meets Jim is made to feel that during their conversation, they are the only person in the world Jim is interested in – and that is a remarkable gift.

Further, Jim is an organiser's dream in terms of modesty and co-operation. Despite his huge status, there were never any tantrums or attempts at rank pulling. If Jim had to walk the track at 06.15 – he walked it without a fuss.

If he had to stand in line with 200 riders to have his helmet inspected, he did so with a smile and waited his turn with good grace and courtesy.

If he was required for a photocall at 08.30 – he was the first one there, waiting for the rest of us to catch up. It's easy to see why Mr Honda thought so much of him.

Finally, Jim is good company. As a guest in our home, Jim is kind, quiet, gentle with children, gracious towards

Still 100% pure racer.